INSPIRATIONS FROM GOD

INSPIRATIONS FROM GOD

GOD IS GOOOOD!

EDITH V. CLAY

J Merrill Publishing, Inc., Columbus 43207
www.JMerrill.pub

Copyright © 2020 J Merrill Publishing, Inc.
All rights reserved. No part of this publication may be reproduced, distributed, or transmitted in any form or by any means, including photocopying, recording, or other electronic or mechanical methods, without the prior written permission of the publisher, except in the case of brief quotations embodied in critical reviews and certain other noncommercial uses permitted by copyright law. For permission requests, contact J Merrill Publishing, Inc., 434 Hillpine Drive, Columbus, OH 43207
Published 2020

Library of Congress Control Number: 2021900119
ISBN-13: 978-1-950719-80-8 (Paperback)
ISBN-13: 978-1-950719-79-2 (eBook)

Title: Inspirations from God: God is Gooood!
Author: Edith V. Clay
Photographs: John Clay, Anthony Clay, Dominique Watson

*This is dedicated first of all to Jesus
for he has given me the words to write,
always close right by my side me
my constant guiding light.*

*I thank him for giving to me
my wonderful caring family,
for they have always been there
to support and encourage me.*

*Johnny, my loving husband,
with me through good times or tests
always proving to me that God
had given me his very best.*

*Our wonderful son Anthony
his wife Erica and son Brian all dear to us,
John, though gone to be with the Lord
Dominique, our dear granddaughter, he left with us.*

*My caring brothers and sisters
couldn't ask for any better,
Lloyd and Vi, Sandi and Bobby, Edith
Pam and Glen, Flo, Bobby, and Etta.*

Whether you call me Momma, Auntie, Edith,
Sis Clay, Mom Clay, Grandma Clay too,
for the love you always show to me
this book is also dedicated to you.

CONTENTS

Introduction	xi
Preface	xv
1. Apostle Latta's Birthday	1
2. A Little Time	3
3. All Christmas Meant	5
4. Anniversary Card	7
5. Another Year - New Year's Eve	11
6. The Ark of the Covenant	13
7. Be the Light	15
8. Black History 2009	17
9. Black History - Music Poem	21
10. Blessed Women of Distinction	23
11. The Blood	25
12. Celebration of Life	27
13. Dandelion	31
14. Detours	33
15. Did you notice	35
16. Dreams	39
17. Dreams and Visions	41
18. The Evidence of His Love	43
19. Extraordinarily blessed	45
20. Fill my cup	47
21. Fortuitous	49
22. God is Gooood	51
23. God understands	53
24. God's Unclaimed Funds	55
25. Going, going, gone	57
26. GPS	59
27. Happy Father's Day	61
28. Happy Mother's Day	63
29. He came to bring us peace	67

30. I'm listening	69
31. I've got this	71
32. If these walls could talk	73
33. In my sister's closet	77
34. It's all in the name	79
35. It's in the praise	81
36. It's in there	83
37. It's time for a change	85
38. Jesus, my Anchor	87
39. Jesus, the "I AM"	89
40. Just don't hit the rock	91
41. Just in case you didn't know	93
42. Letting Go	95
43. Lord help me	99
44. Love	101
45. Marriage	103
46. Most precious God	105
47. Moving forward	107
48. Much more	109
49. My Wings Await	111
50. The Name	113
51. Now it's time to turn the page	115
52. Once more and again	117
53. Only a test	119
54. Only God	121
55. Over the years, churches have changed	123
56. Pentecost	125
57. Prayer of thanks	127
58. The Reason Why He Came	129
59. The Resurrection	131
60. So many things	133
61. Sometimes	135
62. Speak to my heart	137
63. Spiritual blinders	141
64. Standing in the gap	143
65. Stay in position	145
66. Still working on me	147
67. Stuck in the middle	149

68. These Days	151
69. They need to know	155
70. Think of God's goodness	157
71. Time with Jesus	159
72. To Momma and Daddy	161
73. Twenty-Twenty	163
74. Unlimited possibilities	165
75. Wake up, I want to tell you something	167
76. We are fearfully and wonderfully made	169
77. What's in your junk drawer	171
78. Who Is this king?	173
79. You have come this far by faith	175
80. You have to be ready	177
81. Mother Latta's Eightieth Birthday	179
82. Lord, thank you for not letting go	181
Notes	183
Acknowledgments	185
About the Author	187

INTRODUCTION

One day in the early nineties, I asked God to help me talk to my boys.

They were growing up and were getting to the place they were doing things on their own. They were starting to make their own decisions about things. Yes, that's right, they were teenagers.

As I sat down at my computer praying, asking for help, and words started to fill the page. That was the very first poem I wrote. "Letting go."

As time went on and when there were problems or just different situations going on, God would speak to me as I prayed.

Most times, it was during the night hours. My sisters said that was the only time I was still enough.

When my husband's father passed, God spoke to me in the poem "Standing in the gap." This was letting us know that Mom Clay would probably be coming to live with us.

Other times I would just sit and write. It seemed like everything came out in a poem. I started reciting poems in church after I wrote a poem for Bishop Latta. I just handed it to him, but he told me I had to read it doing the service. From then on, I did a poem for many other occasions at Bible Way.

After that, I began to get requests for poems for birthday parties, poetry readings at other churches, and women's meetings. I even did a poem at a cotillion. Most of what I did was at Bible Way or for special occasions for Bible Way.

When my sister Pam would do different programs, she would always have me do a poem. One poem, "In My Sister's Closet," was one that has spoken to so many women that have heard it. It was written for my sister, Pam. But soon after writing it, I found that there were so many women going through something. The poem told of how God was there for what they were going through.

When the poem came about, I didn't realize how saying items she was taking with her came from my sister's closet would touch so many. But telling how God had brought her through so much was a testimony of her trusting God.

Most times, I would be given a title, and God helped me develop the words. I could tell you of so many times I have been awakened during the night, and God would give me those special words. No way I could come up with them without his help.

One program I did, Apostle John W. Stevenson asked me if I wanted to do a CD. He not only produced a CD for me, his son John even helped me get the CD done. That was a blessing. God has been blessing me so much. I have CDs all over the U.S.

I still wanted to put my poems in a book. Being encouraged by my family and friends, I decided it was time. So here we are, standing at another milestone in my life. God has always been such a very important part of my life.

My mom and dad brought us up in the church, so most of my poems will show that I am a living witness of what God can do. He has always been right close. Not only because of the poems but because God is just gooood.

Not only does the poetry speak to me but to other people too. Through sickness, death, problems. God has been right there for me.

I praise God for my family. We have always been close, and during difficult times God brought us closer. God has brought me through a lot.

In my last illness, I found that the years of hearing about Jesus and trusting him made me stronger than I thought. My husband Johnny and I were able to look at the Dr and say no to operations they wanted me to have, and that showed us our faith was strong. Praise God for the faith he had instilled in us. I say us because Johnny and I have been together for over 52 years now.

So you see, God has been a very present help for us both. During my last illness, I didn't have the energy, when I got back to church, to say God is good the way I wanted to.

> Now I can tell you not in a whisper but with a shout, not trying to catch my breath, with that heart beating where it's supposed to beat at 60, not 25, with authority that God is Gooood!

PREFACE

The titles for most of my poems were from a sermon, a special word from God or from someone in my family. I can't count the times someone would hear something and say there's a poem in there somewhere.

I look at all the words and say God is not only gooood but he is amazing. I feel so privileged that he chose me. As I sent what I thought was the last poem into J Merrill Publishing, I asked my husband is this it? He said no and before the day was over I had a new title.

So, I'm still working. There was also something from a sermon that said, And then there's More. I'm expecting more, because God is gooood!

INSPIRATION 1

APOSTLE LATTA'S BIRTHDAY

Today as we pause to celebrate
another birthday with you,
we thank God for his many blessings
and the many years he has given you.

We thank you for being such an example
on your Christian walk,
a man of honor and integrity,
not just a lot of talk.

You've taught us so many things,
and that wasn't just on Sunday,
but the way you lived your life,
and that was each and every day.

You have always stressed prayer
and what having faith can do,
and If we just trust and believe,
God would see us through.

Your sermons have blessed so many
so many lessons you have taught,
and if we didn't learn something from you
we know that it was our own fault.

It's so hard to find someone these days
who has been such an inspiration,
and that's not just here at Columbus Bible Way,
but you're respected throughout the nation.

We hope you feel our love and respect
each time you walk through the door,
and today, as we pause to celebrate you,
we want you to feel it even more.

Now, this may be your birthday,
but we have been blessed too,
God has shared with us all
the wonderful gift of you

INSPIRATION 2

A LITTLE TIME

Needed a little more time
so that we can spend,
a few minutes with the family
before the day comes to an end.

Time to spend with Jesus
reading and learning his word,
not just hearing the preacher
but practicing what we've heard.

Time to spend with that husband or wife
just sitting there in the chair,
but the job may be waiting,
can't be late and you have to get there.

Time to go to the park
or maybe for a ride,
a program at school or church,
and sit with our family by our side.

So many things going on today
and it affects all of our lives,
from the youngest babe to the oldest saint
so many families, children, husbands, and wives.

Young folks don't want to listen to the older ones
but in them, there is so much knowledge,
don't think that they don't understand things
because some didn't go to college.

New innovations all the time
but they can cause disruption,
cell phones, iPads, video games, the internet
can sometimes lead to family destruction.

One thing we need to remember
If we're facing a problem or crisis,
help is only a prayer away
when you call upon Christ Jesus.

Jesus said if my people which are called by my name,
and that means me and you,
would be humble, pray, turn and seek his face
there is so much he would do.

Given, God has given us a little more time
so we're all still here today,
to fellowship and spend time together
and serve him every day.

INSPIRATION 3
ALL CHRISTMAS MEANT

All Christmas meant when I was small
was toys and gifts, and that was all
as I grew older, I learned in church
of the birth of Jesus, and it meant so much.

To think something so special
sent down from above,
not a toy to be broken and thrown away
but a gift of pure complete love.

Some people in the world today
are at a disadvantage,
they don't realize Gods concern for their lives
or the way that he has planned it.

They go on with their life
as though they are sustaining it on their own,
not understanding the love God has for them
or the mercy each day they are shown.

The song says, "go tell it on the mountain,"
but if you think a mountain is too steep,
tell your family, your neighbor, your friends,
tell that lonely person in the street.

That Jesus came that we may have life
and that more abundantly,
and that he gave the ultimate sacrifice
when he died on Calvary.

They need to know more about Jesus
and why we hold him so dear,
tell them he doesn't just show up at Christmas
but he's with us 365 days a year.

If they are in need of a savior
there's one I'd like to recommend,
for Jesus is the gift that keeps on giving
over and over and over again.

The reason we celebrate Christmas
is not for a toy gift or a game,
but because of the birth of a baby
and Jesus is his name.

INSPIRATION 4
ANNIVERSARY CARD

It seems most of my life
you have been there,
and what a wonderful feeling
to know how much you care.

In our younger years
we were never too far apart,
so we were meant to be together
right from the very start.

My brother told you I was older
you said I was too young, but then,
when I really did turn sixteen
God put you back in my life again.

In the years we've been together
we have faced so many things,
but God always brings us through
whatever life's situations bring.

When I think of the things
God has brought us through,
it has made me stronger
because there was always you.

It's hard to put into words
just how much you mean to me,
our life has been so blessed
It's been a living testimony.

I can look at you and see
the love of God in your life,
and I am so very proud
to say I am your wife.

On this our anniversary
I thank you for all you do,
and I just want to say
John Clay "I Love You"

INSPIRATION 5

ANOTHER YEAR - NEW YEAR'S EVE

Another year has come and gone
and we wonder, where did the time go,
whatever way we spent our time
God's mercy to us each day he did show.

So many things happened in our lives
over the past year,
but we can look at each other and say
praise God we're still here.

The world is changing all around us
some people just playing a different role,
no matter how much power they think they have
my God is still in control.

People making New Year's resolutions
but the first resolution came from above,
it came in the form of a baby
what better resolution than love.

One dictionary defines resolution
as a plan for something to be done,
isn't that exactly what God did
when he gave us his only son.

Along with the resolution came promises
they are all in the bible, don't you know,
Jesus sealed it all on Calvary
because he loved us so.

God does not fall short of his promises
like those that come from men,
but all the promises of God
in him are yea and in him amen.

Amen means so be it,
and as our Apostle says, it's done!
We're here through nothing of ourselves,
but Jesus is the reason.

So as this year comes to an end
and we think of all God has brought us through,
we all can look toward heaven and say
Lord, I thank you for all you do
2 Corinthians 1:20-22

INSPIRATION 6

THE ARK OF THE COVENANT

The Israelites went through many battles,
and the Ark was there through them all,
also, there when they crossed the Jordan
and the march around the Jericho wall.

God gave the instructions on how to construct the Ark
to Moses the instructions he did tell,
he was very specific about every aspect
down to every minute detail.

Although Israel had been through the many battles
one day they didn't follow Gods plans,
not going into battle with God in the lead,
the Ark fell into the Philistines' hands.

The Philistines went through so many hardships
because for God they had no respect,
afraid they put the Ark on a new cart to the Israelites, they sent it
back.

Seeing the Ark was back, the Israelites rejoiced
but they still didn't do as God had said,
trying to keep the Ark from falling off the cart,
poor Uzzah, he did fall dead.

The people were so upset and David, he was upset too,
so, he sent the Ark to Obed-Edom's house
until he decided what to do.

For three months, the Ark was at Obed-Edom's house,
and his house was blessed by the Ark being there,
this gave David time to bring the people's minds together
and to commune with God in prayer.

When David saw that Obed-Edom's house was blessed,
he wasn't upset about what happened anymore.
He knew what needed to be done,
no more deaths like on Nachons threshing floor.

When they went to Obed-Edom's to get the Ark,
they carried it the way that they were told,
and this time, it wasn't carried on a cart
but by the poles on God's sacred Ark of gold.

The Israelites were so very happy
shouting, rejoicing, and praising God along the way, because the Ark
was safe back where it belonged
that's why David danced that day.

INSPIRATION 7

BE THE LIGHT

Here we are at the end of another year
and a new one is coming into view,
I thought, the Lord has done so much for me
but then I asked, Lord, have I done enough for you.

Have I told enough people along my way
about what my God can do?
How he can heal their bodies and make them whole
and how he can bring them through.

Each day we are blessed by his goodness
as he keeps us in his care,
don't want to think of what life would be like
If Jesus wasn't there.

The song says, count your many blessings
well, we know that's too impossible to do
by the time we say number one
God's already at blessing one hundred two.

We could never repay God
for all that he has done,
he gave his life for us all
something no one else has ever done.

Our God has unlimited possibilities
that means there is no end,
to the things that he can do
or the blessings he can send.

God can heal your body
and cause the storms to cease,
and when there is confusion
my God can give you peace.

So, when you meet someone
who feels life is not treating them right,
take the time to tell them about Jesus
and you be the light.

INSPIRATION 8

BLACK HISTORY 2009

What a special time
for black history to be celebrated,
because just a few weeks ago
The first black American president was inaugurated

People of every color
watched with so much pride,
some were so overwhelmed
they just stood and cried.

It made you remember
the people who, over the years,
who fought through trials and trouble
hardship, pain, and tears.

For many years now
people have celebrated black history,
and some people still don't understand
its importance to the black community.

They felt it's just another time
that has been set aside,
but they don't realize
that it's a sense of pride.

As children, we learned in school
of great people and their inventions,
but the ones made by black American's
they somehow forgot to mention.

Most of the information about black history
that we were ever told,
concerned slaves and their escape
through the underground railroad.'

In nineteen twenty-six Dr. G. Carter Woodson
just wanted people to see,
there was more that needed to be told
so he helped institute a week of negro history.

Then in nineteen hundred seventy-six
after a presidential proclamation,
the week was extended
and became a month-long celebration.

So many black people and their inventions
so many great strides in history,
that made things better for us all and helped make people free.

We all know of Dr. Martin Luther King
who marched so people would see,
that all people are equal
no matter what color their skin may be.

President Barack Obama
through wars, troubles, even bad weather,
keeps trying to do what he can
to pull this country together.

We are all an important part of God's family
whether you're a sister or a brother,
and in 1st John four and seven says
we all should love one another.

Through good times or through bad
through problems, pain, whatever,
each person can make a difference
and help make the world better.

INSPIRATION 9
BLACK HISTORY - MUSIC POEM

Music has been part of our lives
as adults or when we were small,
at home, at school, or in church
music has touched us all.

We don't have to use our music
to help give us direction,
but slaves used their songs
to help them jump into action.

There were a lot of songs
with many signs and codes,
to help the slaves escape
along some dark, cold roads.

Slaves had to know exactly
what those codes meant,
like if you wade in the water
the bloodhounds would lose your scent.

Music has evolved a lot
but some old spirituals they sang along the way,
like swing lo sweet chariot, and walk with me Lord
are still sung by us today.

The newer songs they sing today
most have good meaning and rhyme,
but some of this modern music I don't understand
and I'm at a loss for words sometimes.

Now I enjoy my gospel
for in good times and hard,
just like in the slavery days
we turn our thoughts to the Lord.

No matter what your music preference
whatever your favorite song may be,
we're so glad you came to join us
as we celebrate music and black history.

INSPIRATION 10

BLESSED WOMEN OF
DISTINCTION

We're the blessed women of distinction
that means we're set apart,
doing something just a little bit different
but the praise comes from the heart.

You see, God has been good to us
and we want you to understand,
that he's going to get the Glory
even if we just wave our hand.

As we come before you
we want you to join in too,
and let everybody know
that God's been good to you.

We may not be running or jumping
but the praise we're going to give,
and we're going to keep on giving it
for as long as we live.[1]

INSPIRATION 11

THE BLOOD

When I think of the cross
and how Jesus died on Calvary.
I know he died for others, too,
but I take it personally.

They nailed Him to the cross
and to think it was for you and me,
but the blood didn't stop way back then;
it still flows today so freely.

It still gives us strength when we feel faint,
and it's there when things go wrong,
it heals our bodies, and it makes us whole,
and the blood will make you strong.

His life he gave for our salvation,
and some people don't even care,
but Lord, I thank you for your precious blood
because that blood makes me an heir.

Heir of that great salvation
that was purchased on Calvary,
now it's up to us to let the world know
that in Jesus, there is victory.

Today as we think about his resurrection,
there's one thing that we all must tell,
that he's no longer in the grave,
but **JESUS** is alive and well.

INSPIRATION 12

CELEBRATION OF LIFE

These days when you think of seniors
you won't find them just sitting in a rocking chair,
but many are busy, some still working
others traveling here and there.

Most feel they have lived a good life
so many milestones they won't forget,
God has blessed them to do so much
and they're still not finished yet.

Can't count the many mountains
That they may have had to climb,
or the many times God has provided
when they didn't have a dime.

When they think about their life
and look at how good God has been,
they're still feisty, minds still sharp
and there's a smile when they remember when.

Each day we all are blessed by God's goodness
with new mercies to see us through,
he doesn't say, sorry I ran out
I don't have enough today for you.

But our God is rich in mercies
and everything else that we need,
and he continues to provide for us all
our God is awesome indeed.

You may not wake each morning
to the sound of a drum or fife,
but to be blessed to see another day
it's a celebration of life.

Time to celebrate knowing Jesus
well, that's a good place to start,
as he sends the blood flowing so freely
in every beat of our heart.

For you are fearfully and
wonderfully made too,
so we're taking the time today
to stop and celebrate you.[1]

INSPIRATION 13

DANDELION

From the time he was small,
my son would bring to me
a perfect dandelion
the first one he would see.

Not a flower wrapped with baby's breath,
nothing that a flower book shows,
but a small yellow flower
more precious to me than a rose.

This flower grows abundantly,
and it's hard to get rid of,
but the one I receive in the spring
is another form of love.

When the seasons start to change,
and things are fresh and new,
the first dandelion my son sees tells me,
mom, I thought of you.

This year it took on a new meaning
because he is no longer at home,
but it said to me, "I love you, mom,"
no matter where I roam.[1]

INSPIRATION 14
DETOURS

I believe detours in our life
are of our own making,
for God will give us leave way
in the paths that we are taking.

My sons say God has planned our life,
and I know Gods plans are sure,
but when we don't follow God's plans,
we mess up, and there's a detour.

Now following God is not always easy
as we have learned from the time we were small,
we run into problems almost everywhere
but God knows about them all.

Problems in school...detour
peer pressure begins...detour
which way shall I turn...detour
will cares ever end...detour

On this road of life
we're bound to have problems,
but let Jesus lead you
for he will help you solve them.

Now, if you hit a dead-end
and that detour sign is there,
don't fret or lose your cool,
just send up a little prayer.

INSPIRATION 15

DID YOU NOTICE

When you awoke this morning,
you were still in your right mind,
some of the things that bothered you
I helped you leave behind.

Did you notice those aches and pains
that you prayed about yesterday,
when you awoke this morning,
I had taken them away.

That health and strength I give you
to make it through the day,
sometimes you don't even notice
as you go along the way.

Yes, I am your Father
and new mercies each day you see,
but sometimes you go along your way
and forget to notice me.

Did you notice the sun was still shining,
even when it was behind the cloud,
but if you take the time to notice
I am the son shining in you out loud.

I give the rain to help things grow,
and some people still get upset,
but you need the things I send your way
even if you don't notice it.

Did you notice when you go through something,
I am right there by your side,
and when you need someone to talk to
in me, you can always confide.

So many things I have done for you
but just ask yourself this,
how many things have I done for you
and you didn't even notice.

We must always remember to thank the Lord
for everything that he has done,
even if you don't notice
before each day is done.

INSPIRATION 16

DREAMS

Alright, come on, wake up
your dream is out there for you,
time for sleeping is over, but
there are things that you need to do

That vision from the Lord
that's been rolling around in your head,
you can't just leave it there
"Write the vision," God said.

When it is written
write it so it can be clearly read,
for sometimes God says one thing,
and we do another instead.

As you get started,
make sure you are aware
that if you leave God out
that dream may just become a nightmare.

Though sometimes it seems
things take a little while,
God's going to make it happen
in his own time and style.

For if the Lord said it,
he's going to see you through it.
You don't have to wonder will he
when he told you he would do it.

There may be roadblocks along the way
you may feel like you're running out of steam,
don't give up, keep on going
it's closer than it may seem.

That dream, that vision
those things you aspire to see,
with hard work and dedication,
will one day become a reality.

Habakkuk 2:2

INSPIRATION 17

DREAMS AND VISIONS

We all have dreams and visions
of things we would like to see done,
and we mothers all have special dreams
for our daughters and our sons.

Sometimes I may go to sleep,
and everything seems alright,
but in my dreams, a familiar face
just may come into sight

I know not if there is a problem
I know not if there is a care,
but I always ask God to help them,
and you know he was already there.

I know God speaks to us in dreams.
I know because he speaks to me,
It may be in word, in song, or poem,
but God's guiding touch, I see.

Dreams may be of a loved one gone on,
and some will make you wonder why,
sometimes the answer may come to you,
and sometimes you just have to cry.

Now there is one dream that won't leave me puzzled
after I've left my final resting place,
for when I awaken, Jesus will be waiting,
and I will see him face to face.

INSPIRATION 18

THE EVIDENCE OF HIS LOVE

when Jesus died on calvary
to save us all to set us free
had he not died just where would we be
that was the evidence of his love

the peace he gives down in my soul
when storm clouds rise and billows roll
he lets us know that he's in control
the evidence of his love

my life is changed by all he has done
he cares for us all like no other one
new blessings each day from heaven above
the evidence of his love
the evidence of his love

INSPIRATION 19
EXTRAORDINARILY BLESSED

Extraordinarily blessed absolutely, I say,
when you serve a God like the one we serve,
who continually makes a way.

From the time that we awake
and view the morning light,
till the time we close our eyes in sleep
and all through the night.

Blessed with all spiritual blessings
that's in a highly favored way,
he doesn't say there's not enough to go around
or today just isn't your day.

Our God daily loadeth us with benefits
and keeps us in his care.
Can you imagine what life would be like
if Jesus wasn't there?.

Some people think that blessed means
just having material things,
but they don't realize the joy
of serving Jesus brings.

Blessed is the man and the woman
who delights in the law of the Lord,
and a church where people come together
and work and worship on one accord.

To share their talents and knowledge
and to a family belong,
because it takes everyone working together
to help make a church strong.

This weekend has been
a special time here at Bible Way,
where we all are recipients
of Gods blessings, each and every day

We've enjoyed singing, praying, preaching,
praising, and many other special blessings too,
but it's not over yet. There's more to come,
so let the praise continue.

INSPIRATION 20

FILL MY CUP

When you ask God to fill your cup,
how big is the cup you want filled up?
Is it a coffee mug that holds a lot?
Or a demitasse that holds just a spot.

Lord fill me till my joy overflows
from the top of my head to the tip of my toes,
let that joy flow freely, like tears from my eyes.
Lord, I want my joy SUPERSIZED!

INSPIRATION 21

FORTUITOUS

One morning as I awakened,
a word dropped in my mind,
I didn't know what it meant
but the meaning I wanted to find.

In the dictionary, it said the word meant
something that happened by chance,
I don't know why it came to my mind
or how it fit in my circumstance?

when different things happen in my life,
I always say its Gods favor,
and oh, the blessings I have received
because of our wonderful Savior.

I thought about all I had been through,
how God had been right there,
to lead, guide, strengthen and heal me
and provide his tender loving care.

You see, it wasn't by chance
that I am still here today,
but God knew all about my life
even before I had a birthday.

*I've expanded my vocabulary
to include that word, "fortuitous,"
but blessings don't happen to me by chance
but because of the love of Jesus.*

*For we know that all things work together for the good of them that
love the Lord.
Romans 8:28*[1]

INSPIRATION 22

GOD IS GOOOOD

When I come before you
and tell you God is gooood,
I'm not just spouting empty words;
I would tell you more if I could.

You see, when I was sick
my voice was not that loud,
but now I can shout it out
praising my Savior, I am so proud.

My God can do anything
he can heal, renew, restore,
just try him for yourself
he can open any door.

God is so amazing
don't be surprised at what he will do next,
new mercies' he sends us daily
you can read about it in his text.

I will never ever grow tired
of telling how he brought me through,
and what he's done for me
he can do the same for you.

So when I stand before you,
I want it understood,
I want everyone to know that
my God is Gooooood!

INSPIRATION 23

GOD UNDERSTANDS

God who sees and understands
and guides me with his healing hands,
and shows me the way that I must go
instead of me wandering to and fro.

He gives me the strength to carry on
when I must walk in paths unknown,
and lets me know to just be still
while he is doing his perfect will.

God, who sees beyond my thoughts
and helps me out through all my faults,
and gives me strength to find my way,
then shows me there is a brighter day.

He wants us all to trust in him
although our pathway seems to dim,
for Jesus' light is shining still
to help us do his perfect will.

INSPIRATION 24

GOD'S UNCLAIMED FUNDS

Sometimes an article may run
that tells of unclaimed funds,
and all of us have checked for our names
to see if our names are one of the special ones.

Some funds may have been left by a family member
that we knew nothing about,
some could be from a bank account
money you may have forgotten to take out.

Then I began to think about Jesus
and considered all he has done,
how he's always there when we need him
what about God's unclaimed funds.

Like the faith, we sometimes forget to use
for that healing from above,
and when we think nobody cares
what about his wonderful love.

That peace when there is nothing but trouble
and joy when we think there's just rain,
and his arms that he wraps all around us
when it seems there's nothing but pain.

We must always put our trust in Jesus
he'll help with whatever we need done,
and when you think that you have nothing;
just tap into God's unclaimed fund.

INSPIRATION 25
GOING, GOING, GONE

Let me tell you about someone
who can make your problems disappear,
not by hiding them in a basket
or putting them in your ear.

He won't put them in some box
so you think they're gone, and then,
just when your back is turned
they suddenly reappear again.

You can give your problems to Jesus,
whether large, medium, or small,
he doesn't need an assistant
he's big enough to handle them all.

Just tell him about your problems,
you don't need a telephone,
then sit back, relax, give God praises
for they're going, going, gone.

INSPIRATION 26

GPS

Do you know we all have a GPS system
and it doesn't have a cost
because Jesus is a present help
for the sin-sick and the lost.

So many times, we think that we
can do things on our own,
but Jesus knows where we are headed
when we must face the unknown.

When answers seem to take a while,
and we grow tired of waiting,
we mess up trying to do things ourselves,
but Jesus is already recalculating.

That manmade GPS can sometimes
send you in the wrong direction,
but God won't send you anywhere
that he doesn't provide protection.

Our system once sent us traveling
on a road that was treacherous,
hills, curves, valleys, no guard rails,
but my God protected us.

God wants us to keep moving forward
with no manmade U-turns along the way,
for we walk by faith and not by sight
that GPS will guide us every day.

Just what does that GPS stand for
although sometimes we don't deserve it,
blessings, love, mercy to us daily
It's God's Personal Service.

INSPIRATION 27

HAPPY FATHER'S DAY

Today as we celebrate Father's Day,
first, we honor Jesus the Father to us all,
the one we can always count on
and he hears us when we call.

Each morning when we awake,
he sends us his wonderful love
and blessings upon blessings
from his heavenly home up above.

He wanted us to have guidance
from the time of our birth,
so, he gave us fathers and mothers
with a presence here on earth.

Fathers were put here for their children
but he never leaves you when things go wrong,
he's there to help when you need him,
and he always shows himself strong.

Whether you are called Father, daddy, papa,
whatever name you might go by,
you have the best role model to follow
Jesus, our heavenly Father on high.

Now some of us miss our fathers,
for they may no longer be with us,
but we still have someone we can turn to
Father, Daddy, Provider JESUS.

Today as people honor their earthly fathers
there's one thing we all need to do,
give thanks to our heavenly Father and say,
Lord Jesus, we love you.

INSPIRATION 28

    HAPPY MOTHER'S DAY

As I thought of Mother's Day,
so much went through my mind;
mothers give so much to us,
blessed be the ties that bind.

Mothers were set aside as special
to give birth, nourish, and to love,
by the best role model, there could be
Jesus in heaven up above.

They are counselors when there are problems
doctors to help heal, hurts and pain,
teachers, chauffeurs, coaches, friends
there to dry tears that sometimes fall like rain.

Yes, mothers take on so many roles,
for there is so much that they do,
and when a father may be absent,
some take on that role too.

They try to be there for their children
to teach them wrong from right,
and to remind them to trust in Jesus
even when they are out of sight.

Just in case you are blessed enough
to have your mother still here on earth,
then let her know how important she is
you know how much she's worth.

For all those "other mothers,"
who are always there to share
their love and time with the rest of us.
God bless you for being there.

There need not be a given time
or even a given day,
just know that mothers are special
in God's eyes every day.

INSPIRATION 29

HE CAME TO BRING US PEACE

Even before Jesus' miraculous birth,
the purpose has been the same,
to show the world how much he cared
and to save them from sin and shame.

From the time that he first made man
with the freedom to use their own mind,
man has messed up and fallen short
and peace they could not find,

In the days of Noah, Abraham, and Moses,
the prophets and the disciples too,
people were in need of a savior
someone to see them through.

Looking at all that was going on,
God decided to intervene,
so he robed himself in human flesh
and came upon the scene.

He came to earth as a baby
right down from heaven above
our very own personal Savior,
the wonderful gift of love.

He didn't stay a little baby
one day, he died on Calvary,
to save the world from sin and shame,
and that includes you and me.

It seems some people have forgotten
about the real meaning of Christmas,
they are so wrapped up in so many other things
they forget about the birth of Jesus.

They run around from store to store
looking for that special toy, gift, or phone,
only to get frustrated and tired
when they find all of the bargains are gone.

You see, he came to bring us peace
in a world filled with confusion,
it says so in his word
and his word is not an illusion.

Some still looking for that perfect gift
well, it's already been given to us,
wrapped in peace and so many wonderful things,
and the card attached says
Love, from Jesus

INSPIRATION 30
I'M LISTENING

Sometimes I feel like Jesus is saying,
child what is your worry now,
didn't I say I would bear your burdens?
didn't my word show you how?

Didn't I take you through other problems
and show you how to bear them all?
Don't you know I will stand up in you?
Child, trust me, I won't let you fall.

Each time you've asked, I've been there,
and I have never failed you yet.
When will you see I'm always with you?
Or next time, will you also forget.

INSPIRATION 31
I'VE GOT THIS

God didn't second guess himself
when he said let there be light,
he just spoke it into existence,
and he knew that it was right.

When he made the mountains and the valleys
and separated the sea from dry land,
he either spoke it or formed things
with his mighty powerful hand.

He decided to make man
even knowing what he would do,
but he knew that if there were problems,
he'd be there to see us through.'

When it came to our redemption,
he didn't just send someone else,
but he robed himself in flesh
and took care of it himself.

As he hung upon the cross
for the sins of all mankind,
he didn't say, hey, let me down
wait a minute, I've changed my mind

But he took all of the things
that he knew we would go through,
sickness, sorrow, trouble, pain
he did it all for me and you.

Now when there is a problem,
and something goes amiss,
just feel him in your spirit, saying,
"child, trust me, I've also got this.

INSPIRATION 32

    IF THESE WALLS COULD TALK

If these walls could talk
I wonder what would we hear, maybe the testimonies of saints
gone home
the ones we hold so dear.

Would we hear the many sermons that
have been preached along the way,
most by our precious Apostle?
Sometimes he would preach three times on a Sunday.

Could we hear the voices of deliverance
from the sin-sick and the lost,
and hear the saints praising Jesus
during the ten days of Pentecost.

Would we hear the many choirs
that would lift their voices in song,
and hear the saints shouting and rejoicing
as the Lord showed himself strong.

If these walls could talk
but you must listen with your heart,
and remember that in most of our lives
Bible Way has been an important part.

But some people say churches have changed
they're not like they used to be,
but God hasn't changed; he's still the same
and in Jesus, there is still victory.

For in this house, God is still praised
and his blessings, love, and favor still falls,
but all that happened during all these years
is not confined inside these walls.

Bible Way continues to move forward
concerned about every man, woman, boy, and girl,
with different outreaches like GROWTH, Missions
and Harvest for The World.

It may have been started by Eld Latta
but he's Apostle Latta today,
and he has lived his life full of faith and love
while preaching Jesus is the way.

Then there's our Pastor Tim
who has made up in his mind,
to carry on that great legacy
Blessed be the ties that bind.

He may do things a little differently
on his Christian walk,
but we would still hear God getting the Glory
if these walls could talk.

INSPIRATION 33
IN MY SISTER'S CLOSET

In my sisters' closet
many things you'll find,
some will make you wonder,
some will blow your mind.

In my sisters' closet
so hard she tries to hide,
the things she cannot tell me
the pain she holds inside.

Some hard roads she has traveled
so many tears she has cried,
in my sisters' closet
are the things she holds inside.

But God has been there for her
when everything seemed wrong,
to strengthen and restore her
to heal and make her strong.

Discouraged and downhearted,
just look to God above,
he'll loose the chains that bind you
and fill you with his love.[1]

INSPIRATION 34

IT'S ALL IN THE NAME

When I think of the birth of Jesus,
what a blessed story to tell,
of Jesus, our wonderful Savior,
who they also called Emmanuel.

Emmanuel means God with us
and that's all through the year,
we don't have to wait until Christmas
to feel his presence near.

Wonderful Counselor, Mighty God,
Everlasting Father, Prince of Peace.
So many names, so many titles,
and his attributes will never cease.

Some may ask why so many names and titles
well, what does Jesus mean to you,
can you narrow it down to just one thing?
That he has brought you through.

Shall we say that he's amazing
well, that's a good place to start,
as he sends the blood flowing so freely
with every beat of your heart.

How many know him as a doctor
when on your sickbed you lay,
but Jesus the healer came by
and you're here, right now, today.

Who can say he's been a keeper?
With things happening to the left and right,
but Jesus, the protector, was there
to make everything alright.

Is there a witness of his work in the courtroom?
when the judge you needed to convince,
that's when lawyer Jesus stepped in
and showed you he was your defense.

Has anyone ever been in trouble,
and you wondered, does anyone even care?
No job, no food, no money,
but Jesus, the provider, was right there.

So many ways to describe my Jesus
so much he has done for us,
always right there whenever we need him
he's Emmanuel, God with us.

INSPIRATION 35

IT'S IN THE PRAISE

When we give God praise and worship,
It's letting him see,
you have put your trust in him,
whatever the situation may be.

Praise helps to take your mind off
what you're going through,
those troubles you may face
when you don't know what to do.

In this world, you may have tribulations,
but God said to be of good cheer
because he has already overcome
all the things that you may be facing here.

It's letting God know
you appreciate all that he does for you,
because he's always right there
ready, willing, and able to see us through.

Your praise empowers you,
and it can also make you strong.
It can sometimes take you so high
you may forget things are wrong.

We may send our praises up,
but they will never outweigh
the blessings and the mercy
he sends to us each day.

So, whether it's with a loud shout (shabach)
or the lifting of the hands (yadah)
God deserves all of our worship and praise
no matter what the circumstance.

Acts 16:22-27 (25)

INSPIRATION 36
IT'S IN THERE

The strength we need to make it,
the patience we need to take it,
peace when there is confusion
God's word is not an illusion.

Joy when we're feeling down
a friend when no one else is around,
comfort when there is sorrow
a present help for every tomorrow.

A refuge when there is nowhere to go,
a spirit lifter when you're feeling low,
whatever we need to keep us
Is all in the name of Jesus.

INSPIRATION 37

IT'S TIME FOR A CHANGE

Barack Obama, First Black President

The whole world seems excited these days,
and some folks are acting strange,
because a man came along, looked around,
and said it's time for a change.

It's time to make things better
it's time to get things done,
but he asked everyone to help him
because the job can't be done by just one.

The big inauguration has been planned
dignitaries from far and near will participate,
a parade and parties will mark the occasion,
but there's one thing I just want to state.

Would there even be a world today
if God had not done the same,

he looked at what was going on
and decided it was time for a change.

It was time to make things better
it was time to get things done.
So he manifested himself in human form
to do a job that could only be done by one.

Wise men came from far off places
to see the one who came.
Nature today still proves his existence.
Emmanuel is his name.

No parades, no parties
but gifts they did bring,
to the babe that was lying in the manger
who one day would be king.

No eloquent speech was given to say
what he was going to do,
but one day out on Calvary
he gave his life for me and you.

Yes, the world should be excited
but not just for what's happening today, you know,
but because the birth of Jesus
changed the world a long, long time ago.

INSPIRATION 38
JESUS, MY ANCHOR

Living in this world today,
we all need someone to turn to.
when troubles come in like a flood,
and we don't know what to do.

Yes, we can go to friends and loved ones
and thank God, they may be there,
but what a blessed consolation
to know we can always go to God in prayer.

How amazing is our God
all things in our lives he's already seen,
there, in the beginning, there in the end,
and everywhere else in between.

Just imagine he's with us forever
right there when things go wrong,
a very present help in time of trouble
Jesus, unmovable, secure, strong.

An anchor is someone or something
to keep us grounded and steadfast,
a solid rock that won't slip or drift away
God, my anchor, will always last.

We don't want to put our hope
in something that is not stable,
but our anchor is in Jesus
because we know he is able.

Able to keep us from falling
whatever the problem may be,
and with our hope in Jesus
we already have the victory.

Prayer is our lifeline to Jesus
in trouble, sickness, and so much more,
so, when situations try to press you down,
make sure Jesus is your anchor.

INSPIRATION 39

JESUS, THE "I AM"

Jesus is the "I Am"
in the center of my storm,
to guide, help and protect
and keep me from harm.

The "I Am" is my shelter
when things get a little rough,
when storm clouds rise, and billows roll
the "I AM" is tough.

The "I AM" goes before me
to hold back the waves,
and when things seem at their worse
the "I AM," he saves.

The "I AM" is my strength
when days seem dark and sad,
he picks me up and lights the way
He makes my heart feel glad.

We all must put our trust in Jesus,
for he has never failed me yet,
I've been through storms, wind, and rain,
and sometimes I've gotten pretty wet.

But oh, the joy of knowing Jesus
of being in the master's care,
for in the center of my storm,
the "I AM" is there.

INSPIRATION 40

JUST DON'T HIT THE ROCK

Another day God has given me
seems there is so much to do,
but I know that I can get through it, Jesus,
if I put my trust in you.

I know that as we live each day,
some different things come along,
but I just keep reminding myself
with Jesus, I can be strong.

I've read the account of Moses
leading the Israelites through the Red Sea,
I don't ever want to be like them
and forget how much God has done for me.

Then God told Moses to speak to the rock,
and it would give water to drink,
but the people kept murmuring so much
that it brought Moses to the brink.

Although Moses was a good leader
he wouldn't get to go into the promised land,
because the people made him so angry
he struck the rock with the rod he had in his hand.

God wants us to speak to our situation
just like he told Moses to do,
sickness, sadness, problems, pain,
just trust him; he will see us through.

God has done so much for us
new mercies he sends us each day,
at times like Moses, we don't listen
so, we face extra problems along our way

So as I face another day of my life
in God's blessing, I must take stock,
be strong, be vigilant, hold my peace
and remember, Just don't hit the rock.

Numbers 20: 7-12

INSPIRATION 41

JUST IN CASE YOU DIDN'T KNOW

Just in case you didn't know
or maybe it never crossed your mind.
I'd like to share some black history facts
that I just happen to find.

Like the fact that in the nineteen sixties,
a black man named Otis Boykin,
helped with the invention of the pacemaker
to help one's troubled heart beat steady again.

Then there was Dr. Patricia Bath
a black woman, as a matter of fact,
who invented a tool and a procedure
for the accurate removal of a cataract.

Dr. Daniel Hale Williams
did something not done in the nation,
when in 1893 he performed
the first successful open-heart operation.

Another black man in the 1940's
by the name of Dr. Charles Drew,
worked to establish a modern blood bank
to help preserve blood and plasma too

There were so many more names I could mention,
and oh, it's such a shame,
that we reap the benefits of their labor
and don't even know their name.

Some worked through hardship and trouble
to accomplish what they were trying to do,
but they didn't give up; they kept on working
and made things better for me and you.

Others were killed for their beliefs.
Some were jailed, and some got beat,
not for some terrible crime that they committed
but because of their color or they sat in the wrong seat.

We all know some things have changed,
and yes, we have come a long way,
from slavery to marches, to freedom
and there's a black president in the white house today.

I don't recall in the bible when God made man
that anything was mentioned about color,
but I know in 1 John 4:7 it does say
that we all should love one another.

For we are on this earth together
and we all play an important part,
to live, love, and be kindly affectionate to one another
to look not just at one's color, but to look upon his heart.

INSPIRATION 42

LETTING GO

For years you have wanted your children
to grow big, healthy, and strong
you nourish and care,
and pray they won't go wrong,

you give them what they sometimes want,
even if they don't need
and pray that in that world out there,
they will always succeed.

I don't know exactly what
we mothers are supposed to do
when children grow up like you prayed, they would
and no longer need you

I think of the years I've tried
to teach you wrong from right
and pray that you'll remember what I taught you,
even if I'm out of sight.

Sometimes I wonder, have I been too close
and done too much for you
for there were times I know I've done
the things that I knew you should do,

your lessons, dishes, cleaning your room,
sometimes I took your backtalk.
Many mothers have taken less
and decided to take a walk.

Now we come to the time at hand,
and I don't know where to start
except to say no matter what,
you will always be my heart,

I know you no longer need
the mothering that you got before
one day somehow, the boys left out,
and young men came back in the door.

I've never had to deal with young men before,
but I guess I better start
for I feel you drifting away from me,
and it's fatal to lose your heart,

I was put on this earth to be your mom,
and I'm trying to do the best I can
like it or not, I'll keep working at it
even after you become a man.

Now, after you have read this
and understand what I'm trying to say,
reflect on what I've given you
in my own special way.

And when you don't always agree
with what I'm putting down,
try to understand where I'm coming from
and try not to frown.

For today is the start of the rest of my life,
and I've got to start it right
I would love to have a smile on my face
that lasts from morning till night,

but life is not always that way;
sometimes, it takes you lower than a rug.
So when you see your mother looking low,
please kindly give her a hug.

INSPIRATION 43

LORD HELP ME

Lord help me to grow up in you
to do all the things I know I should do,
like reading my bible and learning your word,
hearing the preacher and practicing what I've heard.

Sometimes my life seems so mundane
because of the sorrow because of the pain.
but in all things, I've been through
Lord, I know that I can depend on you.

I've lost a lot, but you've given me much
so many times lonely, but you gave me that touch
to say I love you, I'm always near
you are my child. Please be of good cheer.

I thank you, Lord, for all I've stated
everything in my life you anticipated,
just like a father, you've taught me to be strong
and I can always lean on you when things go wrong.

But speaking the truth in love may grow up into him in all things which is the head even Christ.
Ephesians 4:15

INSPIRATION 44

LOVE

There are different forms of love
we all experience throughout our life,
love of God, family, and friends
love of a husband or a wife.

We all want someone we can depend on
a love tried, true, and sure,
to lift our spirits and make us smile,
a love that will endure.

Having someone, you can lean on,
and help if things go wrong,
to walk by your side and encourage you
the right kind of love will make you strong.

A walk in the park on a sunny day,
a touch that says you care,
it doesn't have to be a whole lot
love sometimes is simply being there.

Yes, we know we can lean on Jesus,
but it was also part of God's plan
that a man should not be lonely
that's why he made a woman for a man.

When that special one knows Jesus
and talks with him each day,
so many things can be accomplished
when you take the time to pray.

If by chance you are blessed enough
to find that one true love,
then let them know how special they are
and thank the Lord above.

For love, these days can be so fleeting
it's hard to find a love that's true,
so, before this day is over
take the time to say, I love you.

INSPIRATION 45

MARRIAGE

When it comes to marriage,
first, there must be love and respect,
communication is a must
and that's an absolute fact

You have to work together
to help get things to work out right,
and no matter what anyone thinks,
no person is always right.

Marriage is a lot of give and take
and supporting each other along the way,
and you have to work at it
each and every day.

There will be problems as you go along
some disappointments will happen too,
and you must look to Jesus
to guide and see you through.

Now, if you are blessed enough

to find that special someone, though hard,
let them know how special they are
and give thanks to the Lord.

INSPIRATION 46
MOST PRECIOUS GOD

Most precious God in these last days
who can fathom all you have done,
you are perfect in all your ways
most precious God you are the one.

Your love transcends our imagination
it's there in spite of the way we are,
it reaches deep as the deepest ocean
and goes beyond the highest star.

No words can tell how much you bless us
today your Lordship we do proclaim,
you're there to help each time we need you
you never change you're always the same.

Most precious God you are my refuge
when trouble comes you know what's best,
when I don't know just what I should do
you calm my soul and give me rest.

INSPIRATION 47
MOVING FORWARD

During the time when Christ was born,
the wise men followed the star,
they were determined to find Jesus
though they had to travel so far.

They didn't have the type of transportation
that we all have today,
no planes, trains, or automobiles
to carry them along the way.

The long miles didn't stop them
the Savior they wanted to see,
Herod said when you find where he is,
come back and tell me.

Warned in a dream not to go back,
they ignored what Herod had said,
so they continued moving forward
to find the blessed Savior instead.

Today if you're looking for a savior,
you don't have to travel so far,
for Jesus is ready, willing, and able
to meet you where you are.

He's in the sky above, the earth beneath
the very air that we breathe,
all he asks is that we trust him
and simply in him believe.

In sickness, he will be your healer.
In trouble, he will see you through.
You can call on him for guidance
when you don't know what to do.

He's no longer that little baby,
but he's our heavenly king,
he's wonderful, amazing, marvelous
he's in the songs we sing.

Once you have met the Savior,
your life will never be the same,
but you have to keep on moving forward
in Jesus' precious name.

INSPIRATION 48

MUCH MORE

As a new day dawns and I give God praise
and wonder what today has in store,
I thank God for what he's already done,
and I know today he will do much more.

So many things God has done for me,
and he has opened many a door,
If what you've tried doesn't seem to work,
try Jesus, for he has much more.

Much more love, joy, strength, and peace
more than you could ever hope for,
Jesus died for us that makes us Christ's heirs;
when you serve him, he gives you much more.

Sometimes you may go through problems,
and folk can hurt you to the core,
but God's strength is made perfect when we are weak,
and his sufficient grace is much more.

Unto whom much is given, much is required
and we all have more than we've ever had before,
so we give him honor and lift up his name
and Lord, we praise you more, much more.

INSPIRATION 49

MY WINGS AWAIT

Do the problems of this world
sometimes get you down,
does it seem like those problems
are always hanging around.

Then lift your hands to Jesus
and ask him for his love,
take in all he is sending you
from heaven up above.

Relax and let God handle it
whatever the problem may be,
for God can bring you through it,
and he will set your soul free.

I must learn to wait on the Lord
that's what my bible states,
for I will get my strength renewed
and I know my wings await.

*They that wait on the Lord shall renew their strength;
they shall mount up with wings as eagles.*

ISAIAH 40:31

INSPIRATION 50
THE NAME

When you give your life to Jesus,
you will never be the same,
there is so much that you receive
when you accept that precious name.

When you take on the name of Jesus,
his blessings will never quit,
and every time you put your trust in him,
you reap another benefit.

You can call on the name of Jesus
whatever you are going through.
It can revive, restore, renew
there is no secret what God can do.

The bible says at the name of Jesus,
even demons will have to flee,
and we know he will be there for us,
whatever the situation may be.

If you need healing, it's in there
peace, love, joy, new mercies each day too,
all he asks is that we trust him
and he will bring us through.

We have a point of contact
that's when you go to him in prayer,
and when you call upon that name,
just know he will be there.

When we say we have the name of Jesus,
we must wear it proudly,
you see,
just look at the price that he paid
when he died on Calvary.

We must never take it for granted
the love he has shown for us,
and we must let the whole world know
there is power in the name of Jesus.

INSPIRATION 51

NOW IT'S TIME TO TURN THE PAGE

Now it's time to turn the page
but first, you must open the book,
for so many things in God's word
deserve another look.

Sometimes, you may read a scripture
and one meaning you happen to find
read it again in a day or two
another meaning may come to mind.

Sometimes the words may not be
as clear as we want them to be,
and it's hard to figure out
how it relates to you and me.

Some scriptures may come as a teaching
as you're trying to figure things out,
some may come through a preacher,
something you never thought about.

But oh, when you read the word
and let God speak to your heart,
it stirs up something deep inside
that was right there from the start.

God's word is so powerful
when you let it sink in,
it can renew, restore, deliver
and save people from their sin.

It goes all through your spirit
something you couldn't buy with the highest wage,
you say, Lord, I thank you, now I understand
now it's time to turn the page.

INSPIRATION 52
ONCE MORE AND AGAIN

Once more and again
I come to you in prayer,
to thank you for all you've done
and for always being there.

I see your mighty hands at work
in all things that surrounds,
and if my eyes are closed
Lord, I hear your mighty sounds.

To walk, to talk, to breathe
are blessings you daily send,
thank you, Lord, for everything.
You've done it once more and again.

INSPIRATION 53

ONLY A TEST

It's only a test no need to worry
was the one thing that came to my mind,
it will all be over in an hour,
or two,
everything will be just fine.

Sometimes things don't happen as planned.
The doctor said there was a problem,
but we know that when problems come,
go directly to the one who can solve them.

Thank God for my praying family,
for they all knew what to do,
they called on the name of Jesus
and today, I stand here before you.

For God sent a special blessing my way,
and I thank him for what he has done,
not that I was so deserving

but for that blessing, I was the one.

It had my name on it
just as plain as it could be,
and though other blessings came down,
this one came directly to me.

We don't know why some things happen,
why troubles come or billows roll,
but when you put your trust in Jesus,
you know who's in control.

INSPIRATION 54
ONLY GOD

In a time such as this
when hearts are joined in prayer,
to ask God for his tender love
and to keep you in his care.

We saw how much you were going through,
and sometimes you tried to smile,
to us, it seemed like an eternity
but to God, it was just a little while.

God knew how much we loved you,
and we knew he loved you too,
but it was still hard for us to understand
all the things you were going through.

We look at where God has brought you from,
and some people still may not understand,
but we know the healing that was taking place
couldn't be done by a mortal man.

Only God can work on the heart
and start it over and over again,
and yours was meant to keep on going
and it won't stop till God says when.

Today we smile as we look at you,
and we will for many more days;
he left you here to be a witness
and continue to sing his praise.[1]

INSPIRATION 55

OVER THE YEARS, CHURCHES HAVE CHANGED

Over the years, churches have changed,
and you may see a different type of ministry,
but God hasn't changed. His word is still the same –
same message, just a different delivery.

The message may come in the words of a song
through music, puppets, rap, dance, or mime.
But whatever way it comes forth,
it says that God is good, and he's good all the time.

Some churches people attend these days
they go in and just sit quiet,
but here, when the spirit hits you,
you gonna move, you can't deny it.

Prices today are going sky high,
but salvation is still free,
what a privilege to have a church
where God's Spirit can flow so freely.

For in this house, God is praised,
and he's magnified,
he's lifted up for all to see,
and his name is glorified.

In this house, Jesus is the answer
whatever the problem may be,
if you come in broken, you can leave whole,
come in bound, you can be set free.

In this house, the word is given
all are welcome to come and dine,
there are plenty of good blessings to go around
because Jesus is yours and mine.

Psalms one hundred fifty tells
of many ways that we can praise the Lord,
do you know what could happen
if we would get on one accord?

When praises go up, blessings come down
that's one thing I know for sure,
so, I'm going to keep on praising him
'cause I want everything that God has in store.

INSPIRATION 56

PENTECOST

Fifty days after the resurrection
and ten days after he ascended above,
Christ sent down his Holy Spirit
more evidence of his love.

On the Day of Pentecost
when minds were on one accord,
there came a mighty rushing sound from Heaven
the power promised by the Lord.

Now this wasn't any ordinary power
that they were told to wait for,
it filled the whole room where they were sitting
because God always gives you more.

It came as tongues of fire
and it sat upon each head,
they spoke in unknown tongues
but many nations understood what was said.

They were declaring the wonderful works of God
that's what the people heard that day,
and later on, many more souls received that power
after they listened to what Peter had to say.

Sometimes these days it seems so hard
for people to draw their minds together,
they're thinking of so many other things going on
family problems, their jobs, even the weather.

When I think of the things God has done
the many ways he has brought us through,
the fact that he shed his precious blood
just to save me and you.

After doing that he still wasn't finished
he continues to give us more,
and we sometimes forget all we have need of
he's already provided for.

Acts 1:8 says, but you shall receive power
after that the holy ghost is come upon you,
that wasn't just meant for the saints of old
but it was meant for us too.

Power to walk in the newness of life
power to help in all we do,
and we must be witnesses of this power
we must tell other people too.

Tell them that Jesus is alive and well
and that power is still active today,
and it's available to all that believe
when you let him have his way.

INSPIRATION 57

PRAYER OF THANKS

Lord, thank you for this day
and for the light in my pathway.
For protection during the night,
and for making things alright.

For the family that is close today
and for others that are far away,
for the strength, you give to go through
and for all your blessings too.

For guidance, help, and protection
your love that reaches in every direction,
for your mercy help and your grace
to help us in this human race.

For everything you send from above
And especially your undying love,
I give you thanks as my day begins
In Jesus' precious name. Amen

In everything, give thanks for this is the will of God in Christ Jesus concerning you. 1 Thessalonians 5:18

INSPIRATION 58

THE REASON WHY HE CAME

Before his birth, over 2000 years ago,
Jesus purpose has been the same,
and he has proven down through the years
the very reason why he came.

He came that we may have life
and that more abundantly,
not so people would get so stressed out
trying to put presents under a Christmas tree.

Those special gifts you want to give
to help spread Christmas cheer,
may cost more than you have to spend
some may be still paying for gifts purchased last year.

Everyone likes to receive presents,
but material things soon fade away,
but Gods wonderful gift of mercy
is renewed each and every day.

As I thought about gifts and presents,
God brought this thought to mind,
in his presence is fullness of joy
and so much more you can find.

My God is omnipresent
everywhere for everyone at the same time,
and his love doesn't cost anything
not even one thin dime.

With so much going on today,
it has been a different year,
people are wondering what's going to happen
and where do we go from here?

Well, Jesus is still the reason for the season,
and every other season of the year,
our purpose is to continue to tell about Jesus.
That's where we go from here.

This year as you celebrate Christmas,
send some praises up above,
and give thanks for the birth of Jesus,
that wonderful gift of love.

INSPIRATION 59

THE RESURRECTION

A friend said a profound question hit him
one morning as he got out of bed,
do people really believe in the resurrection?
If so, Why do some act as though God is dead?

Could it be the lives they are living
that makes people seem so lost,
or are some people just so busy
they sometimes lose sight of the cross.

The fact is Jesus laid down his life
in that sad, dark ninth hour,
but he didn't stay dead; he rose again.
Now that's resurrection power!

Had there not been a resurrection
then the world would have no hope,
no way for them to be set free
no way for them to cope.

Not only did Jesus rise again
but he gave us power too,
power to walk in the newness of life
power to help in all we do.

I know that there was a resurrection
for every word of God is true,
and those who die in Christ, when he returns,
then we shall have a resurrection too.

INSPIRATION 60

SO MANY THINGS

If I were to try to recount
the things God has done for me,
so many wonderful things
some I don't even see.

If I would have started yesterday,
he was already into today,
helping me with what I needed
and continually making a way.

If I were to think about tomorrow,
he was already down the road,
still taking care of me
and carrying my load.

So let me try to take a moment
to say just some of the things God has done…like

Waking me up, giving me peace,

clothed in my right mind,
eyes to see, breath to breathe,
and the lord does it all the time.

Strength, love, joy, peace,
my loving friends and family,
hope for tomorrow, joy in sorrow,
a church to worship freely.

Hands to write his loving thoughts,
a mind to get things straight,
God's wonderful word to teach me
and to show me how to wait.

A place to sleep, food to eat,
clothes to keep me warm,
and so many times, I didn't even know
he's protected me from harm.

Understanding, healing faith,
and I could go on and on,
but I must stop and take my seat
because my moments are gone.

INSPIRATION 61
SOMETIMES

Sometimes problems in our life
keep us bound and tied,
and it's hard to let things go, believe me,
I know I've tried.

But oh, when you take the time to pray
and let God take control,
we can relax and praise his name,
for he's watching over our soul.

The more I praise, the stronger I grow,
for God inhabits our praise you see;
the more I keep my mind on Jesus,
the more my soul is set free.

INSPIRATION 62

    SPEAK TO MY HEART

This morning when You rose
and started on your way,
I gave you brand new mercies.
Are you listening to what I say?

When you asked me to help you,
I hear each time you pray,
my Holy Spirit I sent to guide you,
what more can I say.

I sent my word as a guiding light,
and that was only just a start
when I gave my life on Calvary
I was speaking to your heart.

I'm always there to help you;
my word will show you how,
but you've got to listen to what I'm saying.
I wonder, are you listening now.

For he says

I'm in the trees though they stand still.
I'm here to help you do my will,
I'm in your heart. I'm in your home.
You can take me with you; I even roam.

I'm with you when things go wrong
I'm always there to make you strong,
I give you peace, I give you love
I give you help from up above

I'm in your storm, I'm in your rain,
I know your fears; I feel your pain,

and if you think I am not there,
then think again, I'm everywhere.

I am your guide to give you protection,
I'm the fence around you, I'm your protection,
I'm in your night, I'm in your day
I'll teach you how to walk, for I am the way.

I'm with you in joy and in sorrow
I am your hope for every tomorrow,
and sometimes when you think I'm not there,
don't despair, for I'm here, I'm there, I'm everywhere.

INSPIRATION 63
SPIRITUAL BLINDERS

Help me, Lord, when I get to church
that my eyes won't see so much,
I walk into the church, and before I sit down,
I need your peace and your loving touch.

Let me not be so quick to judge some of the things I see,
and let me not be quite so upset,
when someone seems a little short with me.

When there is a problem,
and it shows upon my face,
help me so I won't complain
but give me some shut-mouth grace.

If there is something that doesn't seem right
just let my heart be a little kinder,
and on each side of my head,
please place a spiritual blinder.

INSPIRATION 64
STANDING IN THE GAP

Lord for those who are sick
and have not the strength to pray,
and cannot lift their hands to you
and thank you for their day.

For the old and the young
whose minds are gradually slipping away,
some don't even remember their names
as they face another day.

For those in the streets that feel
there's nowhere they can go,
they walk around with pain in their hearts
stumbling to and fro.

For those who are well,
have a home and the mind to pray,
but neglect to take the time
to thank you for their day.

For all the others who are hurting
and don't have eyes to see,
that you are there and answer prayer
and always will be.

For the younger ones who act as though
they don't really care,
but they've heard of a risen savior,
and they know that you are there.

For all your people everywhere who sometimes give God a bad rap,
give me faith, patience, and love
to always stand in the gap.

Ezekiel 22:30

INSPIRATION 65

STAY IN POSITION

Whatever your situation
when there's something you must do,
you have to stay in position
and God will see you through.

Just know that you are covered
by the precious blood of Jesus,
and there's no place we can go
that God will not be with us.

So as you go on your way
know he's right there by your side,
and the words you need to say
the lord will be there to provide.

INSPIRATION 66
STILL WORKING ON ME

I think I have the name Clay
so I will remember to see
that I am on the potter's wheel,
and God's still working on me.

Now when problems and trials come,
and I don't know what to do,
the wheel turns, and he reminds me,
child, I'm still working on you.

Sometimes things press in around me,
and it's like I'm in a kiln,
but God can take me through the fire
when I put my trust in him.

Clay has to be kneaded and molded
into the shape you want, you see,
so Lord, I just want you to mold me
make me what you want me to be.

INSPIRATION 67

STUCK IN THE MIDDLE

When we pray about something, in the beginning,
we know God will make it alright in the end,
but Lord, I keep getting stuck
in the middle again, and again and again.

There's something about getting things worked out
that seems to take a little time,
but I know that if I leave it with Jesus,
he will work things out just fine.

So next time I have a problem,
I will stop making God so little,
I'll pray and let God handle it
then I won't get stuck in the middle.

INSPIRATION 68
THESE DAYS

In the bible days, they called it a plague
these days, it's called a pandemic,
whatever you want to call it
so many people have died or gotten sick.

Pharaoh didn't want to listen
to what God sent Moses to say,
and seeing what's going on now,
some people are not listening today.

We see everything that's happening,
and there is much unrest in the land,
but no matter what it looks like
everything is still in God's hand.

If my people who are called
by my name and that means all of us,
would humble themselves and pray
we would see the power of Jesus.

There's more that we must do
that some people still don't understand,
we must seek His face and turn from wicked ways,
then he will hear and heal the land.

There are so many people
that are still leaving this world,
this virus doesn't care who it takes out
be it man, woman, boy, or girl.

As we awake and face another day
God's loving mercies we see,
when you make God your habitation,
he said no evil shall come nigh thee.

There are some who have forgotten
that God is still in charge,
since their lives are run by their greed
as their bank accounts enlarge.

You see, our God is so amazing,
and he said to be of good cheer,
for he has already taken care of
what we may be facing here.

In his own time, God will show
what his word already records,
he is the blessed and only potentate
the King of Kings and Lord of Lords.

2 Chronicles 7:14 If my people, which are called by my name, shall humble themselves, and pray, and seek my face, and turn from their wicked ways; then will I hear from heaven, and will forgive their sin, and will heal their land.

Psalms 91: 9-10 Because thou hast made the Lord, which is my refuge, even the most High, thy habitation; There shall no evil befall thee, neither shall any plague come nigh thy dwelling.

I Timothy 6:15 Which in his times he shall shew, who is the blessed and only potentate, the King of Kings, and Lord of Lords.

INSPIRATION 69
THEY NEED TO KNOW

As this year comes to an end
and a new year comes into view,
I know what God has done for me
but I ask Lord have I done enough for you?

Have I told someone along my way
about what my God can do
how he can lift their burdens and make them whole,
and how he can bring them through.

Well, the song says, "Go tell it on the mountain,"
but if you think a mountain is too steep,
then tell your family, tell your friends,
tell that lonely one in the street.

That Jesus came that we may have life
and that more abundantly
and that he shed his precious blood
when he died on Calvary

They need to know more about Jesus
and why we hold him so dear,
tell them he doesn't just show up at Christmas,
but he's with them 365 days a year.

And if they are in need of a savior
there's one I'd like to recommend
for Jesus is the gift that keeps on giving
over and over and over again.

Your own personal Savior
and he's our heavenly king,
he's wonderful, amazing, marvelous
my God can do anything.

If you're sick, he will be your healer.
In trouble, he will see you through.
You can call on him for guidance
when you don't know what to do.

You see, he is always right close;
you don't have to look so far
for Jesus is ready, willing, and able
to meet you just where you are

Once you've met the blessed Savior
your life will never be the same;
all he asks is that we trust him
and praise his holy name.

INSPIRATION 70

THINK OF GOD'S GOODNESS

When I think of the goodness of Jesus
may not be written in the bible that way
but oh, it's all through the word
just expressed in a different way.

David in so many of his psalms
talked of the goodness of Jesus,
and so many things he thanked God for
are things that also relate to us.

In Psalms 8, David said when I consider
that means to think carefully about
all that God had done or made,
of God's excellence, he had no doubt.

Psalms 34 says to magnify the Lord
that means to make him large,
so as we pray and draw him closer
he shows us that he is in charge.

Psalms 145 says I will extol thee
that's praising him to the highest,
and when we take time to do that
that's thinking of his goodness.

Psalms 31 talks of his great goodness
he has laid up for them that trust him
and hallelujah, his goodness is still there
even when things seem a little dim.

Psalms 8 says that God visiteth man
and oh, what a consolation to see,
that when he died out on Calvary
that he was thinking about me.

INSPIRATION 71

TIME WITH JESUS

Six days before the Passover,
Jesus went to Bethany,
to visit Mary, Martha, and Lazarus,
friends whom he loved dearly.

He had raised Lazarus from the dead along
with many other miracles, he did do,
like healing the sick, making the lame to walk,
and opening blinded eyes too.

The Disciples and others were with Jesus at Martha's;
they would fellowship and eat.
Martha felt like she was doing all the work
while Mary sat at Jesus' feet.

Martha was so very busy
doing work over here and over there,
she felt she was doing what needed to be done
but did anyone else really care?

Martha asked Jesus to make Mary help her.
She was doing all the work on her own,
Jesus said she is doing what is needed
"that is far better, don't bother her. Leave her alone."

Sometimes we like Martha
get so busy with so much we have to do,
our homes, families, so many other things,
but Jesus continues to see us through.

The message in the story
that this scripture is trying to tell us,
no matter how busy our lives may become
like Mary, we need to spend more time with Jesus.

INSPIRATION 72

TO MOMMA AND DADDY

It's still so very hard for me
to realize how long you have been gone,
my last talk with you I had,
was over 40 years ago on the phone.

You were getting ready for church
you called to see if the boys were alright,
I didn't know at that time
what would happen on that night.

Your retirement dinner, the family had planned,
but soon tears would run down my face,
a drunk driver took your lives that night,
and you retired to another place.

You had lived your lives for Jesus
and showed everyone God's love,
now you're resting safely with him
in that heavenly home above.

Those memories of you, Momma and Daddy,
are so very special to me,
for you taught us the Love of Jesus,
for this was your legacy.

INSPIRATION 73
TWENTY-TWENTY

Twenty-Twenty has been a different year.
it's one we won't soon forget,
COVID-19, financial hardships, civil unrest,
and the year is not even over yet.

This year has been so strange.
We all have had to face different tests,
but with all that has been going on,
we can still say we have been blessed.

Celebrating along with Apostle and Mother Latta
60 years of faith, love, and trust,
we may not be able to gather inside.
But we are still rejoicing in the name of Jesus.

Pastor Tim, you have reminded us.
We must keep our trust in Jesus,
that the building is just brick and mortar
and the church is inside of us.

We all know that you have had
some different decisions to make,
and you continue to seek God's guidance
because you know people's lives are at stake.

One question we know you face weekly
service in the parking lot or online,
but wherever you choose to bring God's word
the message is always right on time.

Being a pastor is not always easy
so many people with so many problems,
you say keep praying and look to Jesus
because he is the one that can solve them.

Eight stands for new beginnings
and as you trust him more and more,
you said you can't wait to see
the many things God has in store.

Today as we honor you
We honor Lady Yolanda too,
for she has been there with you
in the many things you have had to go through.

With all the many changes this year,
there's one thing that still remains true,
as you keep standing for Jesus
we're still standing with you.

INSPIRATION 74

UNLIMITED POSSIBILITIES

Unlimited possibilities
that means that there is no end
to the things that God can do
or the blessings he can send.

Some people may not know
of the power of the Lord,
but we know you can ask God anything
to him, there is nothing too hard.

Unlimited faith, power, healing,
peace, joy, and love,
all of this and so much more
from our Father up above.

Such an amazing God we serve
to be able to care for us all,
no other God even has the power
to hear us all when we call.

When you go to God for something,
he will never ever say,
all the blessings are gone
there is not enough for you today.

Take the limits off (one songwriter said),
but we keep putting them back,
and not fully trusting him
is it more faith that we lack?

Unlimited means having no restrictions,
no boundaries or controls,
knowing our God can handle all things,
for he cares for our souls.

All of his blessings are unlimited,
and they always will be the same;
all he asks is that we trust him
and praise his holy name.

INSPIRATION 75

WAKE UP, I WANT TO TELL YOU SOMETHING

Wake up, I want to tell you something
I'm still here, but you're getting too busy again,
too much time doing other things
as a new day you begin.

You thanked me for your day this morning.
Yes, you did take time for that,
for food, family, health, even water
and other things you didn't forget.

You stopped and read a short scripture
before you rushed out of the door,
was that enough to start your day?
I was waiting for just a little bit more.

So many things I have brought you through
It's all because I love you so.
So many things I've done, you can't tell others about
because you don't even know.

The blood's still running warm in your veins,
and you often remark, "I'm still here,"
just remember to work out your salvation
with trembling and with fear.

Not that you have to stop doing
so many things that I see,
but while you're so busy doing other things,
remember, some of that time belongs to me.

INSPIRATION 76

WE ARE FEARFULLY AND WONDERFULLY MADE

We are fearfully and wonderfully made,
and that includes our color too,
for no one else can make a man
the way my God can do.

His color chart goes from the whitest white
and to the darkest hue,
for no one else can color the world
the way my God can do.

We're all the same on the inside
just covered by different shades of skin;
some may be white, some may be dark,
and some may be a blend.

In Genesis, when God made man,
there was nothing said about color,
but in 1st John 4:7, it says that
we all should love one another.

No matter what the color
we're related through and through,
for no one else can make a world
the way my God can do.

INSPIRATION 77

WHAT'S IN YOUR JUNK DRAWER

Maybe a piece of paper
that should have been thrown away,
but it had a coupon on it
and I may use it one day.

A black piece of plastic
that should have been gone,
but I had to save it somewhere
one day I'll glue it back on the phone.

Many different pieces and parts
a lot of this, that, and the other,
put in the corner of the drawer
some of it belonged to my mother.

A funny shaped piece of cardboard
torn off a box from the store,
should have been gone but left it there
it keeps the overflow from falling on the floor.

When thinking about my Christian walk
and the way I live my life,
I wondered what's in the back of my mind
that could cause pain and strife.

That painful memory that lingers, still,
that doesn't seem to go away,
I thought it was gone but to my surprise,
it showed back up again the other day.

So many things in the back of my mind
that sometimes makes me feel sad,
need to be forgotten and thrown away
and replaced with God's word instead.

Lord clean my heart, my mind, my soul.
I want you to straighten out the place,
but don't just stop there; please renew my joy
and fill me with your loving grace.

INSPIRATION 78

WHO IS THIS KING?

Who is this king who loved us so
that he left his throne in Glory,
to save us all from sin and shame
but that's just the tip of the story.

He did not come dressed
in fine attire or long royal robes,
but he came as a babe so meek and mild,
and they wrapped him in swaddling clothes.

Who is this king who always knew
what was in store when he became a man
but that didn't stop him; he pressed his way on
for he had a perfect plan.

He did not stay that little babe
that babe grew up to be
the wonderful king who would give his life
so that you and I could be free.

Who is this king? He's El Shaddai, The Mighty God,
the Prince of Peace and so much more to us,
and no matter what name you call him
I like to call him Jesus.

We must always remember that wonderful birth
but not just at Christmas, you see,
but we must thank the Lord all year long
for the gift of love, he's given you and me.

He does not ask for cake or candles
like those used to celebrate the day that we were born,
but today I say light the candles toot the horn for
Jesus Christ, The Wonderful Savior, The King of Glory, is born.

INSPIRATION 79

YOU HAVE COME THIS FAR BY FAITH

The bible says

The days of our years are threescore and ten
that adds up to seventy,
and if by strength eighty
there's even a few of you we see.

You have come through many situations
trusting God to see you through,
and showing people along the way
what faith in God can do.

You have taken on many roles and titles
and so much love you have shown,
not only to your own family
but others too when they were in need or alone.

Who can find a virtuous woman?
Well, we have a few here today

who have lived your lives for Jesus
and been examples every day.

Some may think you haven't done much
that you have just lived your lives,
but you all have been witnesses that whatever you need,
God always supplies.

Your life is a living testimony
just look at the lives you did touch,
and in case you haven't heard it, lately
you are appreciated very much.

Seasoned by the word of God,
whatever problems may beset,
you have come this far by faith,
and you're still not finished yet.

As we look at the beautiful women of God,
each one special in your own way,
and all deserving of the accolades
that you are receiving today.

INSPIRATION 80
YOU HAVE TO BE READY

You don't have to be old when it's time to leave this world,
but we still don't understand it when death takes a boy or girl,
sometimes the unexpected happens, and we don't know just why,
but we all know that in this life, it is appointed for us to die.

You don't have to be sick, a person can feel really good,
and they could be living just like a good Christian should,
then unexpectedly one day there's a call on our phone
the voice says there was an accident, and your loved one is gone.

Such an eye-opening experience that people can be gone so fast.
But this earthly house of this tabernacle was not designed to last,
for we are only here for a short time. We will all leave this place,
so we need to make sure we're prepared to meet God face to face.

You have to be ready, and that means each and every day
you must keep your mind on Jesus and continually watch and pray,
for a person can leave this world at any time, life can go so fast, but
if we're ready when he calls our name, we'll have eternal life at last.

Jesus has been getting us ready from the time we were small,
always there to guide us because he's concerned about us all.
So if we follow his instructions and continually praise his name,
we will be ready to go with him the day he calls our name.

Hebrews 9:27
II Corinthians 5:1

INSPIRATION 81

MOTHER LATTA'S EIGHTIETH BIRTHDAY

Even before you were born
God had plans for your life,
even the fact that one day
you would be our Apostle's wife.

So many things concerning you
were already set in place,
and just think all this was done
before your mother saw your face.

Your many years of Christian service
and helping others along the way,
shows the love of God in your life
and we honor you today.

You not only cared for your own children
but you picked up a few others too,
God wanted someone who would be faithful
that someone Mother Latta was you.

You have been such a help to so many
when answers we needed to find,
and someone we could confide in
when there were things on our minds.

With all your many accomplishments
and all you have come through.
You could say (drop the mic) I've done enough
but God still has plans for you.

There are still so many people
who need to hear your wisdom from the Lord,
and see that they can make it
although sometimes it gets hard.

I know that you would tell people
whatever may come their way,
to put their trust in Jesus
and you just have to pray.

Having an eightieth birthday
may be hard for some people to face,
but you need to take a bow
for you have done it with style and grace.

Today as we celebrate with you,
we pray that you have more abundant love,
and blessings upon blessings
from our father up above.

INSPIRATION 82

LORD, THANK YOU FOR NOT LETTING GO

Lord, thank you for the children
that you put in our care,
and for teaching us how to love them
and for always being there.

Tony has always been our quiet one
reading, finding out what things were about,
at the church that he attends
he helps other people out.

John was our adventurer
he was always on the go,
liked being around friends and family
and he loved his daughter so.

We didn't know that one day
when he thought his life was back in tune
that he would be taken from us
still in our hearts, but gone too soon.

Dominique, our granddaughter
on her own, but we're still close to her,
she knows that if she needs us
that we will be right there.

Felecia has called me Momma for years,
Brian and Gabi call me Grandma Clay,
as do Cynthia, Jane'hia, and Royalty
added blessings along the way.

Over the years of raising our children
we went through so many different things,
but Jesus was always our help
in whatever situation life brings.

Our children go through many things
some questions will never be answered,
why we just found out a couple of years ago
what really happened to their pet hamster.

Being a parent is a privilege
just as being a caregiver is too,
someone else's life is put in your care
and God is saying he can depend on you.

We thank the Lord for his constant care
for the love that he does show,
for being a parent to all of us children
and for never letting go.

NOTES

10. BLESSED WOMEN OF DISTINCTION

1. My sister Pam asked me to write something for this group that she started, to let people know, no matter how old you are, you can still do something to give God praise.

    The group has ministered in Churches, nursing homes, special black history programs, and other special occasions around the Columbus area. The group range in age from 63-95.

    Leader Pam Bell, Dollie Trent, Patricia Stevenson, Florence Black, Vivian Price, Rowena Whitney, Shirley Jennings, Ella Carroll, Beverly Hairston, Etta Taylor, Viola Dillard, Edith Clay.

    Manager Glen Bell, Assistant Felecia Cook - Special remembrance Margaret Board

12. CELEBRATION OF LIFE

1. Written for Eva M. Bailey and ended up being a poem about our precious senior saints. I have had people read it and say that's about me.

13. DANDELION

1. ** Written for my son Tony. He is 46 now but I still get my dandelion in the spring.

21. FORTUITOUS

1. Was it fortuitous that my brother and Jackie's dad met over 60 years ago?

    And Jackie Jr. became the publisher of my book.

    I say again, nothing happens by chance but, God knows the plans he has for my life.

33. IN MY SISTER'S CLOSET

1. Written for my sister Faye (Pam) when she was going through some difficulties in her life. It let so many sisters know through it all God will be there for them just like he was for her.

54. ONLY GOD

1. Written for my brother Lloyd when he was in the hospital and things kept happening but God was in control. He is still with us and singing to the Glory of God.

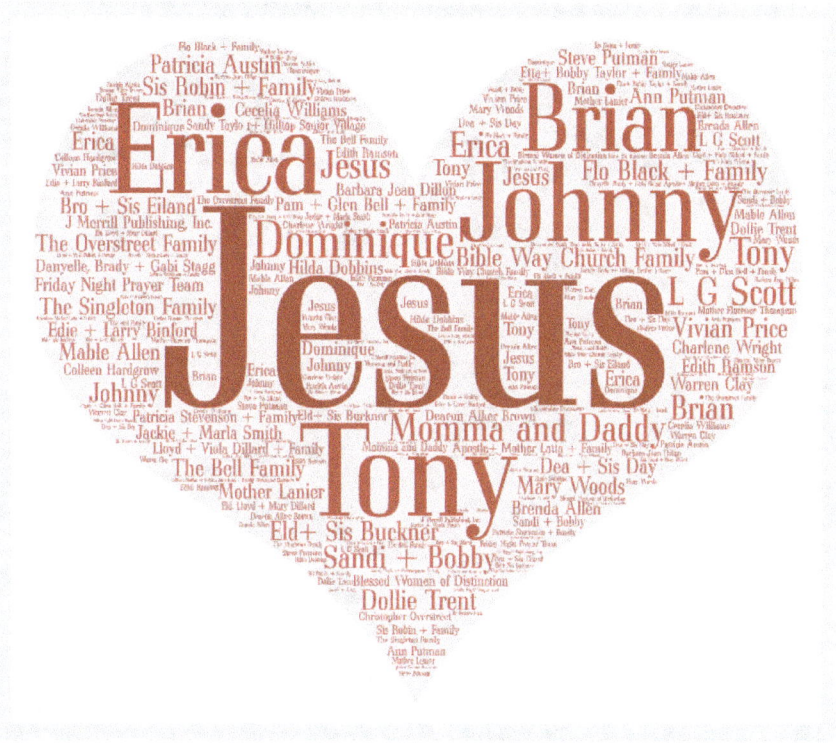

This is a special thank you first to Jesus
for all he has done for me,
for the people he has put in my life
that mean so much to me.

Couldn't list all of the names
there were so many to say thank you to,
just in case you don't see your name
this space is reserved especially for you.

.

ABOUT THE AUTHOR

Edith V. Clay was born in West Virginia. Moved to Columbus with her parents. Graduated from West High School, soon after she married her husband John. They had two boys. John and Anthony. She began writing poetry in the 1990s. It was doing different times and situations in her life, that God gave her words of inspiration and she started to write them down. She found that the poems were not only encouraging to her, but to others that heard them too. Most of the poems were about God, church, family, and friends, all so very important in her life.

www.ingramcontent.com/pod-product-compliance
Lightning Source LLC
Chambersburg PA
CBHW072008110526
44592CB00012B/1235